# RUNNING

AN INSPIRATION

ALI CLARKE

summersdale

RUNNING

Copyright © Summersdale Publishers Ltd, 2014

All rights reserved.

No part of this book may be reproduced by any means, nor transmitted, nor translated into a machine language, without the written permission of the publishers.

Condition of Sale
This book is sold subject to the condition that it shall not, by way of trade or otherwise, be lent, re-sold, hired out or otherwise circulated in any form of binding or cover other than that in which it is published and without a similar condition including this condition being imposed on the subsequent purchaser.

Summersdale Publishers Ltd
46 West Street
Chichester
West Sussex
PO19 1RP
UK

www.summersdale.com

Printed and bound in China

ISBN: 978-1-84953-615-8

Substantial discounts on bulk quantities of Summersdale books are available to corporations, professional associations and other organisations. For details contact Nicky Douglas by telephone: +44 (0) 1243 756902, fax: +44 (0) 1243 786300 or email: nicky@summersdale.com.

# INTRODUCTION

Running isn't a hobby – it's a way of life.

Perhaps you took your first tentative jog down the road with a hint of scepticism, or maybe you struggled through your first few long-distance runs, but the odds are, if you're reading this, you've got the running bug.

Whether it's the excitement of seeing your stamina increase over time, the challenge of beating personal records or the sheer exhilaration you feel as your feet pound the pavement and the wind rushes by, every runner has that one thing that fills them with joy and keeps them coming back for more. You can't necessarily describe the feeling that a good run gives, but you know you want to experience it over and over again.

But running is not all fun and games; whether you're aiming to complete yet another ultramarathon or the track around your local park, training your body and pushing it further than it has gone before is hard, and it takes mental as well as physical strength to carry on when the going gets tough. You need motivation, determination and commitment to succeed, and that's where this book comes in.

These pages, filled with inspirational photos, quotes and mantras, will fire you with the encouragement you need to get out there – and once you reach your finishing line and feel the adrenaline rush through

EVERY DAY

——— IS A GOOD DAY ———

WHEN YOU RUN.

NO MATTER HOW SLOW YOU GO,
— YOU ARE STILL LAPPING EVERYBODY —
ON THE COUCH.

WHETHER IT'S A 14-MINUTE MILE
——— OR A 7-MINUTE MILE, ———
IT IS STILL A MILE.

# ONE DAY, THIS WILL BE YOUR **WARM-UP**.

# THEY SUCCEED, BECAUSE THEY THINK THEY CAN.

## VIRGIL

*On good days I run.*
# ON BAD DAYS I RUN LONGER.

STRENGTH DOES NOT COME FROM
PHYSICAL CAPACITY. IT COMES
FROM AN INDOMITABLE WILL.

MAHATMA GANDHI

IT'S NOT ABOUT HOW BAD YOU WANT IT.
—— IT'S ABOUT HOW HARD YOU'RE WILLING ——
TO WORK FOR IT.

I COUNT MY SUCCESS

—— IN MILES, ——

NOT POUNDS.

THERE IS NO SUCH THING
——————————————— AS A ———————————————
REGRETTED RUN.

# FAILURE WILL NEVER OVERTAKE ME IF MY DETERMINATION TO SUCCEED IS STRONG ENOUGH.

OG MANDINO

YOU DON'T HAVE TO GO FAST; YOU JUST HAVE TO GO.

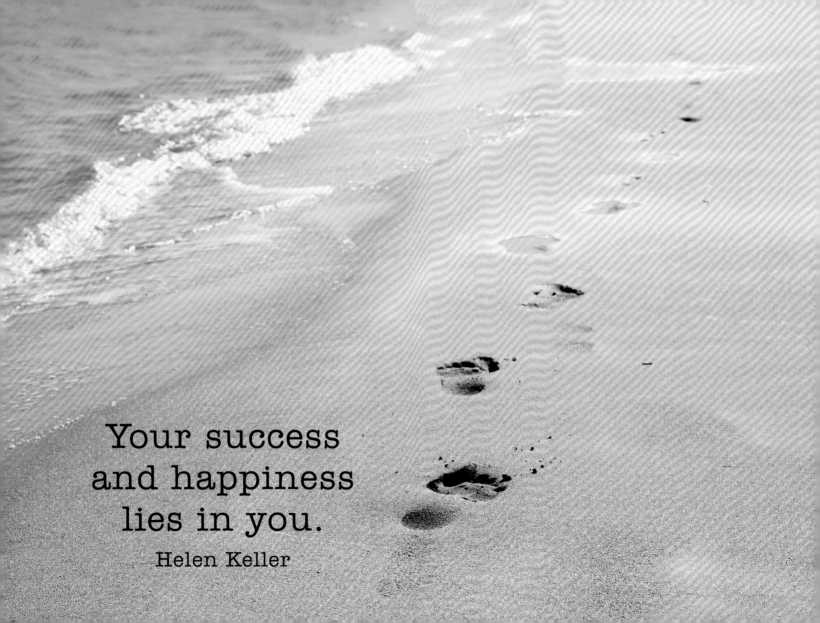

Your success
and happiness
lies in you.
Helen Keller

—— RUN WITH YOUR HEART, ——
# NOT YOUR MIND.

GO AS LONG AS YOU CAN,

—— THEN TAKE ——

ANOTHER STEP.

I RUN BEST WHEN I RUN FREE.

STEVE PREFONTAINE

YOU DON'T HAVE TO BE GREAT
TO START BUT YOU HAVE TO
START TO BE GREAT.

ZIG ZIGLAR

DON'T SIT AROUND WISHING YOU WERE RUNNING.
GET OUT THERE AND **DO IT**.

PAIN IS JUST WEAKNESS
LEAVING THE BODY.

— WORRY LESS. —
# RUN MORE.

STRENGTH AND GROWTH COME
ONLY THROUGH CONTINUOUS
EFFORT AND STRUGGLE.

NAPOLEON HILL

THE MOST CERTAIN WAY TO
SUCCEED IS ALWAYS TO TRY
JUST ONE MORE TIME.

THOMAS EDISON

# THE MIRACLE ISN'T THAT I FINISHED BUT THAT I HAD THE COURAGE TO START.

JOHN BINGHAM

NO, YOUR LEGS AREN'T TIRED. YES, YOU CAN BREATHE.

SLEEP LONGER. EAT BETTER. RUN FASTER. AIM HIGHER.

# BE HAPPIER.

PERSEVERANCE IS NOT A LONG RACE; IT IS MANY SHORT RACES ONE AFTER THE OTHER.

WALTER ELLIOT

IF IT DOESN'T CHALLENGE YOU,

—— IT DOESN'T ——

CHANGE YOU.

START BY DOING WHAT IS
NECESSARY; THEN DO WHAT'S
POSSIBLE; AND SUDDENLY
YOU'RE DOING THE IMPOSSIBLE.

ST FRANCIS OF ASSISI

EVERY TIME YOU ARE READY TO GIVE UP,
—————— A BREAKTHROUGH IS ——————
ABOUT TO HAPPEN.

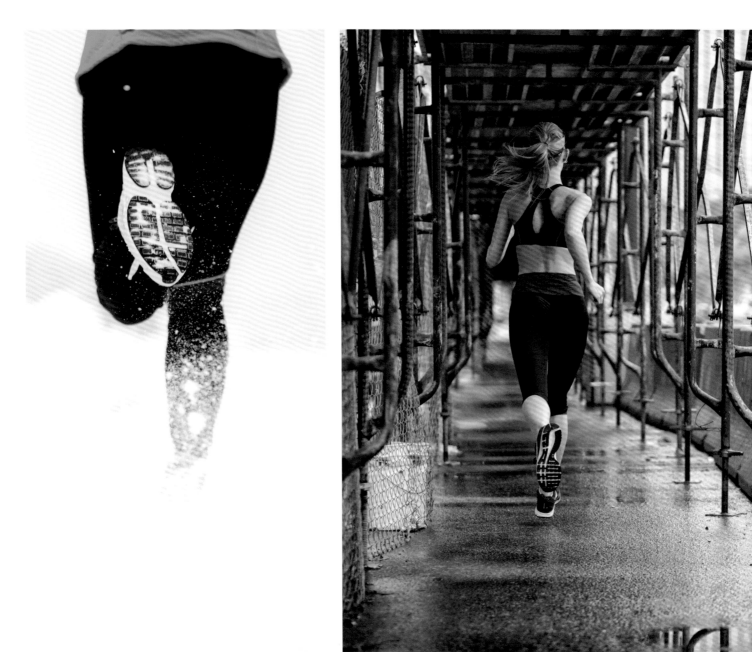

# DON'T DREAM OF WINNING.
# TRAIN FOR IT.

MO FARAH

Find a place inside where there's joy, and the joy will burn out the pain.

Joseph Campbell

WE ARE ALL
RUNNERS.
SOME ARE JUST
FASTER THAN
OTHERS.

Bart Yasso

—————— MOST OF THE TIME, ——————
RUNNING IS THE ANSWER.

YOU'LL NEVER KNOW YOUR LIMITS
—— UNTIL YOU PUSH YOURSELF ——
PAST THEM.

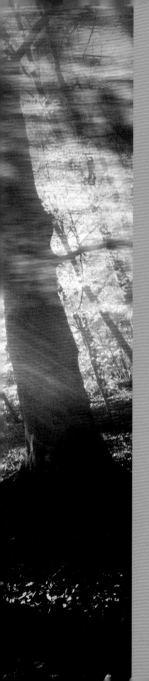

SUCCESS ISN'T A RESULT OF
SPONTANEOUS COMBUSTION. YOU
MUST SET YOURSELF ON FIRE.

ARNOLD H. GLASOW

SOMEONE WHO IS

——— BUSIER THAN YOU IS ———

RUNNING RIGHT NOW.

TODAY'S PAIN IS TOMORROW'S STRENGTH.

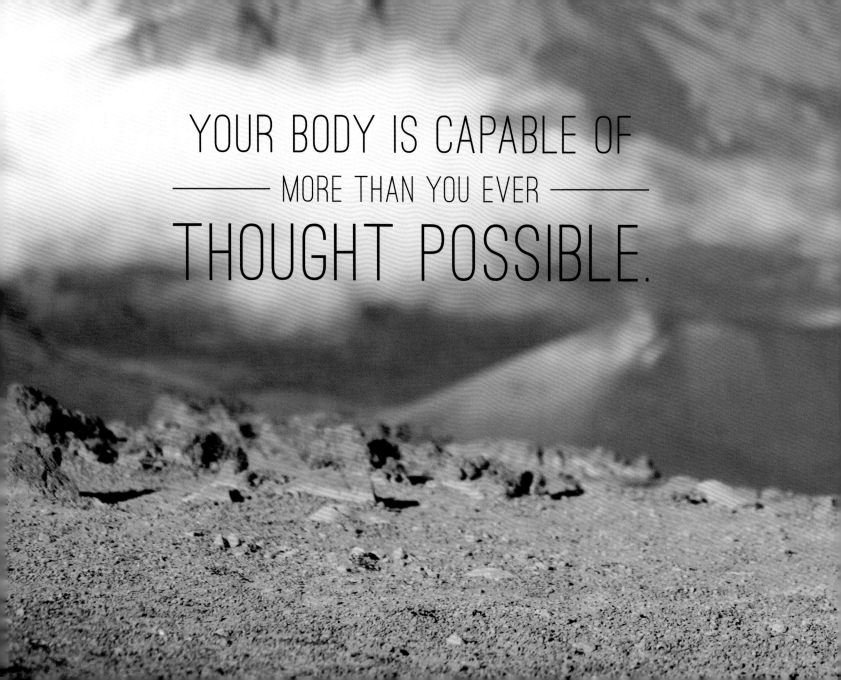

A JOURNEY OF A
THOUSAND MILES BEGINS
WITH A SINGLE STEP.

LAO TZU

A DREAM DOESN'T BECOME
REALITY THROUGH MAGIC; IT
TAKES SWEAT, DETERMINATION
AND HARD WORK.

COLIN POWELL

—— START STRONG. ——
FINISH STRONGER.

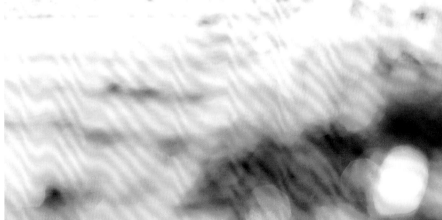

# I DO NOT RUN TO ADD DAYS TO MY LIFE. I RUN TO ADD **LIFE TO MY DAYS**.

Ask yourself, 'Can I give more?'
The answer is usually 'Yes'.

Paul Tergat

## RUNNING IS
## MY THERAPY.

MY MINDSET IS: IF I'M
NOT OUT THERE TRAINING,
SOMEONE ELSE IS.

LYNN JENNINGS

RUN UNTIL IT HURTS,
———————————— AND NEXT TIME ————————————
IT WILL HURT LESS.

THE BEST THING ABOUT RUNNING
IS THE JOY IT BRINGS TO LIFE.

KARA GOUCHER

# IT'S NEVER TOO LATE TO BECOME
# WHAT YOU MIGHT HAVE BEEN.

GEORGE ELIOT

SOME DAY YOU MAY NOT BE ABLE TO RUN.
TODAY IS NOT THAT DAY.

RUNNING IS LIFE

—— WITH THE ——

VOLUME TURNED UP.

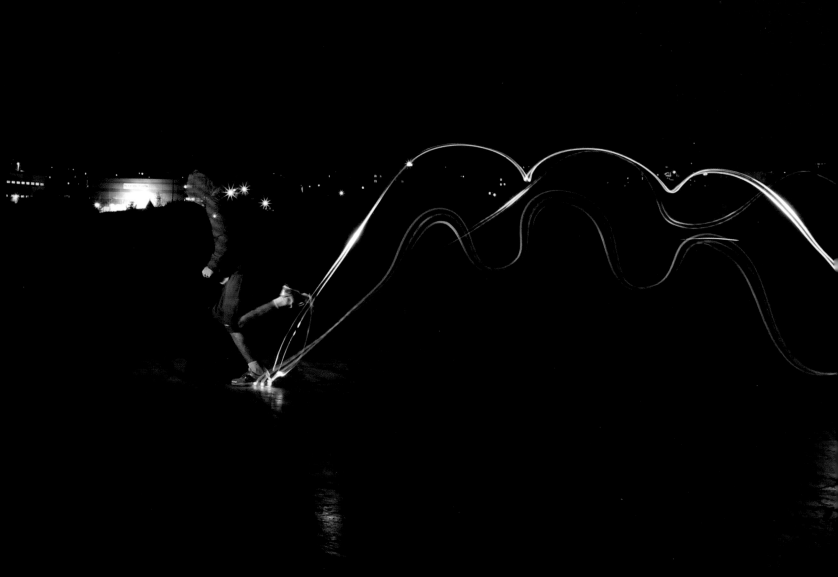

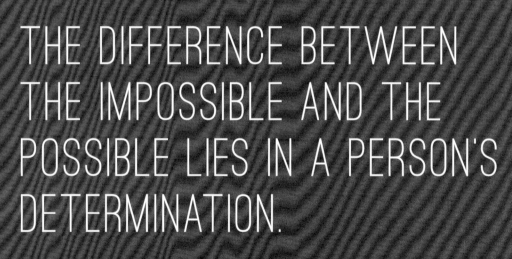

THE DIFFERENCE BETWEEN THE IMPOSSIBLE AND THE POSSIBLE LIES IN A PERSON'S DETERMINATION.

TOMMY LASORDA

THERE IS ONLY ONE RUNNER IN
THIS RACE, AND THAT'S ME.

GEORGE SHEEHAN

WHEN YOU DESPAIR AT HOW FAR
—— YOU HAVE TO GO, THINK OF HOW ——
FAR YOU HAVE COME.

I MAY NOT BE THERE YET, BUT I'M **CLOSER** THAN I WAS **YESTERDAY**.

RUNNING
SETS YOU FREE.

PERSEVERANCE,
SECRET OF ALL
TRIUMPHS.

*Victor Hugo*

SUCCESS IS NOT
—— A DESTINATION: ——
IT IS A JOURNEY.

DON'T WAIT FOR THE PERFECT CONDITIONS.
———————— IT'S ALWAYS THE ————————
PERFECT TIME TO RUN.

WHEN THE WORLD TELLS ME
—— I'M WEAK, RUNNING TELLS ME ——
I'M STRONG.

WITH THE NEW DAY COMES NEW
STRENGTHS AND NEW THOUGHTS.

ELEANOR ROOSEVELT

GET UP. LACE UP. SHOW UP. NEVER GIVE UP.

DON'T BEAT YOURSELF UP IF YOU MISS A RUN. REMEMBER:

REST DAYS ARE IMPORTANT TOO.

*Running is*
QUALITY TIME
WITH ME.

ACCEPT THE CHALLENGES
SO YOU CAN FEEL THE
EXHILARATION OF VICTORY.

GEORGE S PATTON

# ACKNOWLEDGEMENTS

Special thanks go to all of the photographers for providing such fantastic photos – this wonderful book couldn't have been realised without your support.

# PHOTO CREDITS

(In Alphabetical Order)

aaron belford/Shutterstock

Abigail Schellberg

Alberto Rojas Serrano

Ammentorp Photography/Shutterstock

Amy Johansson/Shutterstock

Angela Aladro mella/Shutterstock

baranq/Shutterstock

Blazej Lyjak/Shutterstock

Brett Nattrass/Shutterstock

Carol Drew

catwalker/Shutterstock

Christopher Edwin Nuzzaco/Shutterstock

Clive Harris/www.photosoul.co.uk

CREATISTA/Shutterstock

Dasha Petrenko/Shutterstock

Dennis van de Water/Shutterstock

Dirima/Shutterstock

Ditty_about_summer/Shutterstock

dotshock/Shutterstock

EpicStockMedia/Shutterstock

Eran Hakim

Evan Fitzer

Galyna Andrushko/Shutterstock

Gary Blakeley/Shutterstock

guigaamartins/Shutterstock

Halfpoint/Shutterstock

Iakov Kalinin/Shutterstock

I T A L O/Shutterstock

Jaromir Chalabala/Shutterstock

J. Henning Buchholz/Shutterstock

Jack Newton

JordiDelgado/Shutterstock

Kerem Tapani Gültekin

KieferPix/Shutterstock

Kokhanchikov/Shutterstock

Konstantin Yolshin/Shutterstock

Krom1975/Shutterstock

Leena Robinson/Shutterstock

Leslie Paige for Lake Mead National Recreation Area,
photo courtesy of the National Park Service

l i g h t p o e t/Shutterstock

lightwavemedia/Shutterstock

luckyraccoon/Shutterstock

lzf/Shutterstock

Manczurov/Shutterstock

Marco Rubino/Shutterstock

Maridav/Shutterstock

Mark Stevens

Maxisport/Shutterstock

melis/Shutterstock

mezzotint/Shutterstock

Michal Skowronski/Shutterstock

Mikael Damkier/Shutterstock

msgrafixx/Shutterstock

nature photos/Shutterstock

Nomad_Soul/Shutterstock

ollyy/Shutterstock

Øystein Tveiten/I'm flickring

Paul Sidle

Pawel Krupinski

Phase4Studios/Shutterstock

Photosani/Shutterstock

Pressmaster/Shutterstock

Rafal Olechowski/Shutterstock

Rafal Olkis/Shutterstock

Ratikova/Shutterstock

Rihardzz/Shutterstock

Saddoggdesign/Shutterstock

S.Pytel/Shutterstock

Sunny studio/Shutterstock

TAGSTOCK1/Shutterstock

Tom Wang/Shutterstock

Thomas Kessens/www.thomaskessens.com

Tomas Picka/Shutterstock

Val Thoermer/Shutterstock

Volodymyr Burdiak/Shutterstock

vovan/Shutterstock

Warren Goldswain/Shutterstock

YanLev/Shutterstock

If you're interested in finding out more about our books, find us on Facebook at **SUMMERSDALE PUBLISHERS** and follow us on Twitter at **@SUMMERSDALE**.

**WWW.SUMMERSDALE.COM**